# INTRODUCING

# The Fenderbenders

Dad       Mom       Chrystal      Todd      Maniac

See if *you* can find America's zaniest family in…

# The Fenderbenders Get
# Lost in America
## Again!

### By Holly Kowitt

**SCHOLASTIC INC.**

New York   Toronto   London   Auckland   Sydney

For Harlan and Susan

ISBN 0-590-45891-4

Copyright © 1992 by Holly Kowitt.
All rights reserved. Published by Scholastic Inc.

12 11 10 9 8 7 6 5 4 3 2        2 3 4 5 6 7/9

Printed in the U.S.A.        08

First Scholastic printing, September 1992

Dear Diary,
  Can you believe my family's dragging me on a trip cross-country... AGAIN? Get crucial! Everybody has to go- Mom, Dad, my obnoxious brother, Todd, even our dog, Maniac.

I'm psyched to spend some quality time together. NOT.

  Chrystal

Chrystal's Travel Diary

KEEP OUT

Todd That Means You!

Dear Diary,
  Todd Fenderbender's my name, don't wear it out. I live in Festerville, Ohio, with my obnoxious sister, Chrystal, two 'rents, and one bodacious canine. The good news is, you can catch me partying in Hawaii, San Francisco, Las Vegas, Yellowstone National Park, Nashville

and Niagara Falls. The bad news is, Mom is making me keep this stupid diary. What did I ever do to her?
  Be cool,
  Todd

AGAINST MY WILL

TODD'S DIARY

UNDER PROTEST

NO WAY JOSÉ

BEWARE! MUTANT RADIATION RAYS INSIDE

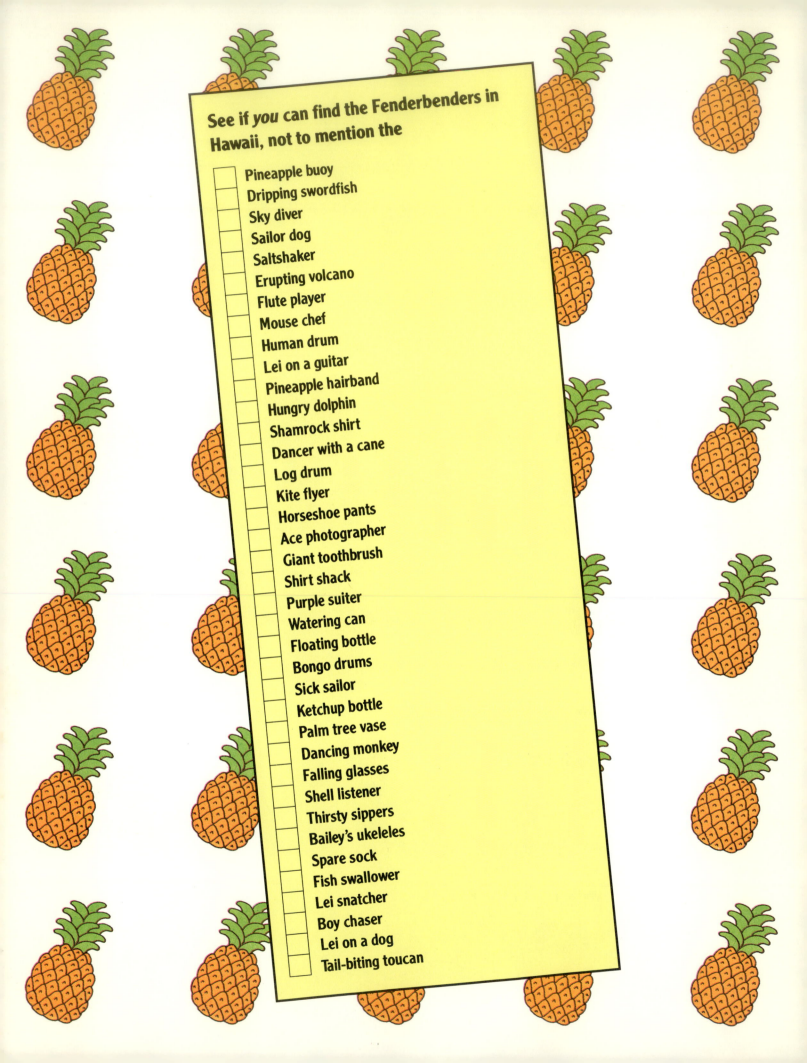

See if *you* can find the Fenderbenders in Hawaii, not to mention the

- Pineapple buoy
- Dripping swordfish
- Sky diver
- Sailor dog
- Saltshaker
- Erupting volcano
- Flute player
- Mouse chef
- Human drum
- Lei on a guitar
- Pineapple hairband
- Hungry dolphin
- Shamrock shirt
- Dancer with a cane
- Log drum
- Kite flyer
- Horseshoe pants
- Ace photographer
- Giant toothbrush
- Shirt shack
- Purple suiter
- Watering can
- Floating bottle
- Bongo drums
- Sick sailor
- Ketchup bottle
- Palm tree vase
- Dancing monkey
- Falling glasses
- Shell listener
- Thirsty sippers
- Bailey's ukeleles
- Spare sock
- Fish swallower
- Lei snatcher
- Boy chaser
- Lei on a dog
- Tail-biting toucan

See if *you* can find the Fenderbenders in San Francisco, not to mention the

- [ ] Pizza delivery boy
- [ ] Fish kiss
- [ ] Butterfly net
- [ ] Fish in a pocket
- [ ] Flying ad
- [ ] Pigeon chef
- [ ] Pagoda phone booth
- [ ] Cowboy hat tipper
- [ ] Pigeon in shades
- [ ] Duck chef
- [ ] Ant in love
- [ ] Bongo drum player
- [ ] Helicopter
- [ ] Hanging dice
- [ ] Golden Gate Bridge
- [ ] Fish barrel
- [ ] Climbing dinosaur
- [ ] Hairdressers
- [ ] Dog and chain
- [ ] Windowsill napper
- [ ] Rooftop painter
- [ ] Falling dumplings
- [ ] Trolley dog
- [ ] Beehive sippers
- [ ] Anchor tattoo
- [ ] Popcorn eater
- [ ] Giant coffee cup
- [ ] Nose-pinching crab
- [ ] Bonsai tree
- [ ] Pagoda dog house
- [ ] Hot-air balloon
- [ ] Worm in chopsticks
- [ ] Painter on stilts
- [ ] Man with six eyes
- [ ] Sushi vendor
- [ ] Rolling sailboat
- [ ] Manhole
- [ ] Canine chimney sweeper

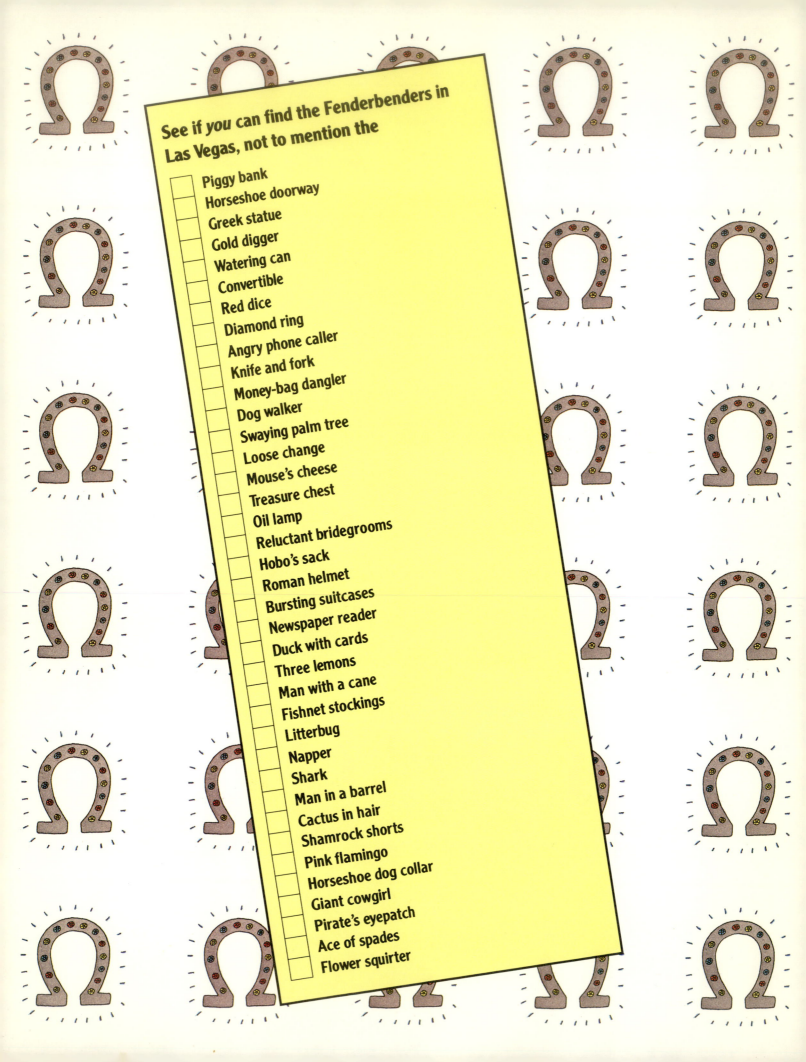

**See if *you* can find the Fenderbenders in Las Vegas, not to mention the**

- [ ] Piggy bank
- [ ] Horseshoe doorway
- [ ] Greek statue
- [ ] Gold digger
- [ ] Watering can
- [ ] Convertible
- [ ] Red dice
- [ ] Diamond ring
- [ ] Angry phone caller
- [ ] Knife and fork
- [ ] Money-bag dangler
- [ ] Dog walker
- [ ] Swaying palm tree
- [ ] Loose change
- [ ] Mouse's cheese
- [ ] Treasure chest
- [ ] Oil lamp
- [ ] Reluctant bridegrooms
- [ ] Hobo's sack
- [ ] Roman helmet
- [ ] Bursting suitcases
- [ ] Newspaper reader
- [ ] Duck with cards
- [ ] Three lemons
- [ ] Man with a cane
- [ ] Fishnet stockings
- [ ] Litterbug
- [ ] Napper
- [ ] Shark
- [ ] Man in a barrel
- [ ] Cactus in hair
- [ ] Shamrock shorts
- [ ] Pink flamingo
- [ ] Horseshoe dog collar
- [ ] Giant cowgirl
- [ ] Pirate's eyepatch
- [ ] Ace of spades
- [ ] Flower squirter

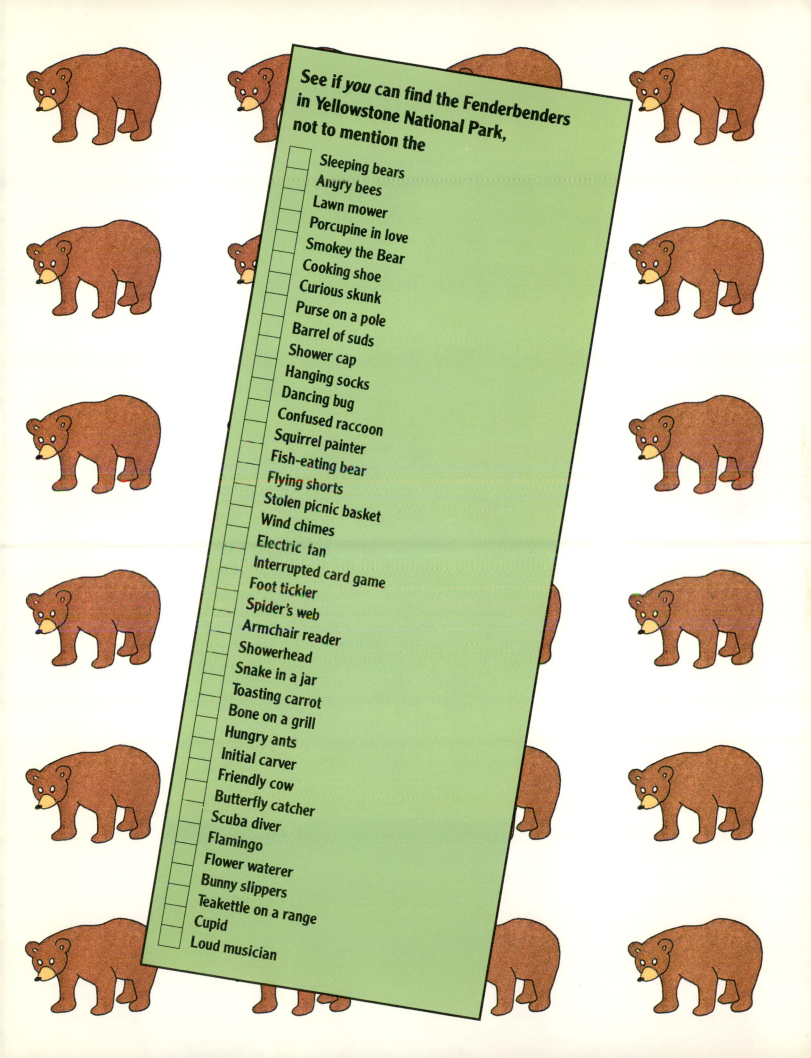

See if you can find the Fenderbenders in Yellowstone National Park, not to mention the

- [ ] Sleeping bears
- [ ] Angry bees
- [ ] Lawn mower
- [ ] Porcupine in love
- [ ] Smokey the Bear
- [ ] Cooking shoe
- [ ] Curious skunk
- [ ] Purse on a pole
- [ ] Barrel of suds
- [ ] Shower cap
- [ ] Hanging socks
- [ ] Dancing bug
- [ ] Confused raccoon
- [ ] Squirrel painter
- [ ] Fish-eating bear
- [ ] Flying shorts
- [ ] Stolen picnic basket
- [ ] Wind chimes
- [ ] Electric fan
- [ ] Interrupted card game
- [ ] Foot tickler
- [ ] Spider's web
- [ ] Armchair reader
- [ ] Showerhead
- [ ] Snake in a jar
- [ ] Toasting carrot
- [ ] Bone on a grill
- [ ] Hungry ants
- [ ] Initial carver
- [ ] Friendly cow
- [ ] Butterfly catcher
- [ ] Scuba diver
- [ ] Flamingo
- [ ] Flower waterer
- [ ] Bunny slippers
- [ ] Teakettle on a range
- [ ] Cupid
- [ ] Loud musician